DEBORAH VIRANT-YOUNG

REFRESH YOUR PURPOSE

MOVING FORWARD THROUGH REFLECTIVE JOURNALING

Refresh Your Purpose
Moving Forward Through Reflective Journaling
All Rights Reserved.
Copyright © 2023 Dr. Deborah Virant-Young
v3.0

The opinions expressed in this manuscript are solely the opinions of the author and do not represent the opinions or thoughts of the publisher. The author has represented and warranted full ownership and/or legal right to publish all the materials in this book.

This book may not be reproduced, transmitted, or stored in whole or in part by any means, including graphic, electronic, or mechanical without the express written consent of the publisher except in the case of brief quotations embodied in critical articles and reviews.

Outskirts Press, Inc.
http://www.outskirtspress.com

ISBN: 978-1-9772-6407-7

Cover Photo © 2023 www.gettyimages.com. All rights reserved - used with permission.

Outskirts Press and the "OP" logo are trademarks belonging to Outskirts Press, Inc.

PRINTED IN THE UNITED STATES OF AMERICA

I went through the roller coaster of life not realizing or honoring my purpose. Every day felt the same (yes, like Groundhog Day!). I was going through the motions, doing the same thing, often times hoping for a different outcome. So, what made those feeling change? I want to share about my journey into "adulting" first and how coaching and journaling **changed my life**. It will help explain more on why I journal every day and why I wrote this book… and show you what changed. I want this book to build you into your "self-coach" that has **YOUR** needs and wants as a priority, because we know that way too often, we put others needs first.

"What is that and do I need it?" was what I said to my friend with tears already running down my checks from anxiety and overwhelm. I was walking through Baby's R' US (in 2011) with her guiding me on the most practical things for my baby shower registry. Thank goodness I had a "coach" to guide me that day or I would have either left the store in hysterical tears with nothing on the registry or would have registered for every gimmicky, latest and greatest, baby and toddler who-knows-what that I did not need in order to keep my child fed (bottles), dry (diapers), clothed, and safe (car seat, baby carrier, and stroller).

Just four years earlier (2007), my soon-to-be husband and I were walking through Bed, Bath, and Beyond, registering for our bridal shower. We walked around that store for close to 3-hours… that was painful. We registered for things that we didn't really need or really even want, but because we had to have things on our registry. We scanned them like we were on Supermarket Sweep… scanning any and everything. Sorry to those that purchased half of it… we returned your gift. We didn't need or have the space for the $150 knife block, the automatic opening garbage can wasn't going to work with the dog, the over-priced silverware actually stained quickly after the first few washes so they were returned for the cheaper set that we still have today (15+ years later). What we needed were the new sheets, towels, and bedding, because at the time, we were still using what I had from my college apartment days. Heck, I still have the laundry basket I received for my high school graduation that was filled with those towels for my college dorm days. Wow… now that I think about it, those towels are also still in our home and used by our kids. Anyways, Jerry and I clearly did not have a "coach" for the bridal shower registry… if we had, we may have registered at more than one store, with the other store being Lowes or Home Depot. We like the more practical things. His favorite gift that I got him to this day is a bucket and window squeegee he fills with windshield washer fluid in the winter that he uses to clean the car windows regularly from the salt and dirt from driving the Michigan winter roads. But those were things we didn't know, think about, or have someone guide us on what we really needed. At that time, we also weren't personally reflective enough to guide ourselves.

When I go back even a little further to my college years, I had advisors but never a coach. Never someone to stand beside me, asking me the tough questions about what I wanted, needed, desired… about who I wanted to be. I was however "advised" on what classes I needed to take, what extracurricular activities I "needed" to participate in. My true passions and what I wanted for my ideal self were never explored with me at the most pivotal times in my life. I was going through a world that was already set in its ways to what was "the norm", what was "expected of me", or to what the "natural progression through life was" and I didn't question it; I didn't have a say in it, and I didn't push back. I did what I thought I "ought" to do in order to meet the expectations of others.

Don't get me wrong, I am very happy with my career, the opportunities afforded to me, the home we have created for our family. And in the process, I had the greatest of mentors that would guide me on my journey. My high school calculus teacher, my WMU BIOS 150 professor (and chair of the department at the time), my U of M College of Pharmacy Infectious Disease Professor and P3-year community pharmacy preceptor, my PGY1 residency director, the chaplain at the hospital during my PGY2 residency, my first "big girl" job Associate Dean at the University, Hospital VP of Nursing when I went back into clinical practice…to recognize a few. These mentors played an important piece in my academic and career trajectory and I am forever thankful. (This might be a good time to reflect on those that had an influence on your life.)

However, I didn't know how to take action on the things I

wanted. All of my adolescent and young adult life, I was on the path of "do as I am told". Even if many of the things and processes I followed *MAY* have been the same I would have chosen for myself, the actual experience would have been very different. I would have wanted to do them; I would have been more invested in the process. But I was doing it because I was told and it often felt like a checkbox to just get it done because I had to. I often didn't explore the "why" behind what I was doing and those that were available to advise/mentor me were not (necessarily) invested in me. Not to say they weren't good at advising because they were. I did everything I was supposed to do, so I was rewarded with positive letters of recommendation, admissions into my doctorate program, acceptance into my 1st year and 2nd year residency programs, my dream career... but something still didn't feel right. I was not as happy as I should have been. I was going through the motions but for what?

I started my journey called LIFE over 40 years ago. There were countless times when I practiced the "all or nothing" approach to EVERYTHING I did. I don't know exactly where I learned that philosophy, but if I wasn't perfect, then I failed and I went back to my old ways, which was really self-destructive to any progress I did make and worse, detrimental to my "potential trajectory" (personal and professional). The one thing I was really good at, was academics. I LOVED learning new things. I was dedicated at "expanding my knowledge" through attending lectures, reading, labs/simulation, and discussion boards/writing. When it came to my healthcare career, I applied everything I leaned in order to provide the best patient care and in my career of teaching future physicians, I love sharing my knowledge and experiences with my students. I love more the opportunities I have in coaching them on become their best self. HOWEVER, when it came to my own care, I could do all the reading and learning the world had to offer and I was still not DOING what I needed to do for MYSELF… for so many years. Or again, would start to but if I wasn't perfect, I failed.

It wasn't until 2019 when I made connection with my personal life coach and in 2021 with my professional coach, where my life changed. In 2019, I was coached for the first time…. It was the first experience I ever had that I had control, that I was part of the decision-making process, that I had a say…. because it was a true partnership of her asking the tough questions and me determining my own action forward, that my ideal self was discovered. I realized very quickly how many aspects in my life I had no control over because someone else was always in the driver seat. Someone else was in that seat because I allowed them to be… I willingly handed them the keys. I was letting many outside forces influence and persuade me into this "ought" self that I had become, without even realizing it. I didn't question it until someone asked me the question of "why….". I had a chance to challenge societal influences on my life and then upon reflecting, I noticed all the other areas in my life where I let cultural beliefs (that I was born and raised into) influence me without even a glimmer of question. Things started to change when I pushed back (just slightly) to allow my true self shine through. During this process I started journaling everyday- reflecting on what I wanted, what I was grateful for, how I wanted to show up (for me and for others) and my life was truly transforming (and it still is). My coach couldn't be by my side every minute of every day, but my journal could be with me at all times… and it was and still is.

I also started integrating the coaching techniques my coach used on me with my own patients, my colleagues, my peers and then, later, in my role as a Director of Faculty and Professional Development, and honestly, with anyone that seeks guidance- my friends, my family, my neighbors. I was no longer telling anyone what they should do, even if they asked me "what would you do?" because quite frankly, what I would do only makes sense for me. It may not make sense or even work for them. We are different people, with different life experiences, and different beliefs, feelings, opinions, and wants in life. I stopped using the infamous phrase, "well, if I were in your shoes…" because in all honesty, I would never be in their "exact" shoes. Our situations would always be different or diverse. I am not the expert in their life, they are. Who was I to tell them what to do? And with that, there was instant success in coaching those around me. Many came back or referred others to me. What they liked about being coached… I didn't tell them what to do. Their self-determined action plan was way more successful than anything I could have told them to do. I could get into the adult learning theory model on why that is but I won't in this book.

During this process, I continued to reflect on other areas of my life and discovered that I needed a coach for things I faced in all my other roles as a: mom/parent navigating the health care arena, despite being a healthcare professional, as well as the education systems, a wife/partner and also, let's not forget a coach for navigating the personal and professional intersection of life as a professional female with competing demands between work and home life. I desired to be well and at peace with my personal and professional life. And when you have a coach, one that is supportive, caring, can push you to the next level, and hold you accountable, you can achieve your goals. So, being well is what I wanted and well is what I am. Don't take this last statement as me saying my life is perfect, because only the social media version of my life looks perfect. Do I have moments where I can't get my S@#$ together, where my kids are pushing just the right buttons to then turn around and tug at those heartstrings that they have full control over, times where my husband and I have different parenting ideas and have conflict in front of the kids, where my professional life is demanding more out of me as I try to continue managing my home/personal life. Hell yes! Life is not easy. It is not greener on the other side. But I also now have a process for navigating the intersection of my personal and professional responsibilities— **journaling**.

It was said by someone, I don't remember who, regarding why do you always take the hard road. And the other person answered "because I didn't know there was another road." Often times we are so in the weeds that we can't even see where we are, where we are going, how we are doing, or that we are even making any progress. We are always looking at how much farther we want to go that we forget to turn around to see how far we have already gone. We need to celebrate our successes more. For each milestone we reach is momentum to keep going.

I sat in on a recent meeting where the question was raised on how we can better address "behaviors" that are concerning-professionalism issues, interpersonal communication gaps, miscues in group dynamic, interactions, and leadership styles. Often the behavioral issues aren't addressed because there isn't as assessment in higher education like there is on K-12 report cards. And those that perform well academically are not receiving additional support from advising or care teams because they aren't flagged as needing support academically. What does an institutions infrastructure look like to provide individuals support? Does one even know the support exists if they are used to not having any support? How can one take advantage of what is offered if they don't know it is available? Furthermore, does one know there is an opportunity for growth if they have never had someone care enough to tell them there is such an opportunity? The best place to start is with self. Self-reflection leads to awareness. Once one is aware, they can make progress toward their goals. Awareness starts with journaling.

The best place to see progress is in the wide-open space. It is like starting on the beach in your row boat and you want to get to the other side of the lake. You start rowing and rowing and rowing. You look forward and see that you have a lot more lake to row across and feel like you haven't made any progress and are never going to get to the other side. Your perspective is wrong. Turn around... look how far you have rowed. You have made progress from where you started. Reflective journaling can bring you out of the weeds into the open water.

I hope that this book will provide some personal perspective through reflective journaling, where you will create your story and discover your strategies that will work for your situation. Journaling will offer you another perspective that you didn't previously think of, as well as let you know that a coach is not that far away and is happy to walk with you on your journey. I am going to share more of my story of how journaling and self-reflection transformed my life. And I am so glad you made the first step in starting your own journey.

Be well!
Deb

In 2019, I was introduced to my personal life coach and pod-caster that spoke the words that I always knew but spoke to me in a way that touched me to my core. My life forever changed. I discovered myself and now, I truly love myself. That was the beginning of my transformation I never thought was possible. Things changed personally for me- I lost weight, the number doesn't matter, because I gained confidence and am still on that journey, I grew closer with my husband of now 15+ years, learned how to better communicate with my children, changed careers, and grew my own coaching business. All of this started, honestly, and simply, by daily journaling. I know, hard to believe.

Many start each new year with a New Year's Resolution. What is it about the first day of the new year that makes us want to "start new"? Also, does it ever really start on January 1st? I can speak from my own experience that it doesn't. Growing up, January 1st was notorious for college football bowl games and what goes with football... boneless wings, mozzarella sticks, chips and dip/salsa, pizza, etc. And then as I got older, it was often the post-New Year's celebration recovery day where I slept in late, rehydrated on the couch as I watched (more) Hallmark holiday movies and (of course) football. So, that New Year's resolution normally didn't start until January 2nd anyways. How is that "starting out the new year STRONG"? I was already making excuses why I couldn't start…. Just this one day won't hurt. I will start tomorrow.

We cannot ignore how corporate America, and I am sure the global economy, has capitalized on our stupidity (collectively) of making a year-long commitment to make a change. And the majority of resolutions revolve around health… working out and eating better. How many advertisements did you see for discounted gym memberships, home gym equipment, weight watchers, and other weight-loss gimics? So, we sign-up with a gumption to "make this year our best year yet". And then never follow through? I saw a meme this year that made my coffee come out my nose… it showed a person that clearly is a regular at the gym, standing and tapping their foot waiting for the "non-gym goer" to be done on a machine, where the "newbie gym goer" was literally just sitting there (not actually using the machine for its intended purpose) and posting pictures of themselves on social media all like "hitting up the gym". The regular gym goer is just waiting for March because by then, all these New Year's resolutioners will be DONE and back to their same ol' same ol'.

But really… we have 365 days to lose weight, quite smoking, earn more money, save money, lose weight, workout more, lose weight, save money… did I repeat myself? So do I realllllllly need to start on day 1 of the New Year… nope… I did the math. So, we already start the new year off on the wrong foot and have ourselves convinced that we can "gamble" with our success.

How am I measuring that success? I am making a 365-day commitment with no way of tracking or holding myself accountable until December 31?!?! So, if it is an improvement to make over an entire year, do you really start on day 1? Most of us play the number game. And here is what it looks like:

> If it is losing 20 pounds, do I really need 365 days to lose 20 pounds? Science says your goal should be to lose 1 pound per week, so I need 20 weeks to lose 20 pounds. Well, 1 year is 52 weeks, so I don't have to start on January 1. Hell, I don't need to start until August! BUT then you are trying to lose those 20 pounds during the next holiday season… you can't win.

You continue to F*%& yourself.

Do we really need to "wait" until January 1st to start new? We have the ability to START NEW with every chance we are given, with every choice we make. Right now is when we start… TODAY. What is the one improvement you can make today or right in this moment that will move you toward your goal? DO that 1 thing… in this moment, right now. How did that feel?!?! Write that feeling down!

A few years ago, I stopped making a New Year's resolution, because why wait until January 1st to make a positive change in my life when I can start NOW, regardless of the date. (I started February 19, 2019). Why wait for a magical day. Start now. Start today. Why put off until tomorrow what you can do today? Go ahead, write down all the excuses you are saying in your head. And then throw them out!

If you troll social media, or have a daily inspiration calendar, you see motivational sayings all around you that may really speak to you and spark something in you to make a change. But what are you actually doing with them? When you re-post it on social media, is it just showing what your goal is, what you should be doing? But then you don't do anything with it? Let's start thinking about how you can put it into action. I have been working at incorporating those self-help, inspirational messages and actions into my daily life and you can too. Normally when I see one that really speaks to me, I use it as my journaling prompt for the next day. I see if by writing about it can spark a change from within. If it does, I go with it. If it doesn't, I move on.

I decided to make this book a workbook for action with writing and journaling prompts for you. This will help with putting those inspirational quotes and memes into action, making it meaningful, as well as productive. Time to move forward EVERYDAY for the next 365 days. It doesn't matter if you are starting this book on January 1st or April 12th, July 4th, September 26th, October 21nd, November 14th, or December 16th… start TODAY!

Reflective writing is a powerful way to reconnect with your purpose. It is a useful way to pause and reflect on an experience and your emotions. In the practice of reflective writing, the stories you write are for the benefit of you, the writer, not the reader, in orer to find meaning in what you do, personally and professionally. It can illuminate tensions at the intersections of personal and professional life and allow you to consider what you need to heal or grow or help you decide what action to take.

I would like to take you on a reflective writing journey of your own for self-growth, self-compassion, and self-love.

Let's do your first reflective writing exercise here. I want you to write a compelling story in just 6 words. Legend has it that Ernest Hemmingway is the originator of the 6 Word-Story when he won a bet. Here is what he wrote:

For Sale: Baby shoes. Never worn.

WOW! That is a gripping story! Emotions are torn in multiple directions with just those 6-words. How did the story make you feel?

____

____

____

Write it down! Your turn. Write your 6-word story!

____

____

____

YAY! It turns out, YOU too can say a lot in just six words.

How did that feel to get those 6 words on paper?

____

____

____

Did it stir up emotion?

____

____

____

Did it spark inspiration?

____

____

____

What are you going to do now with that inspiration?

____

____

____

If you liked the 6-word story, you can use any of the prompts in this book and respond using the 6-word approach or you can write more if the prompt inspires you to do so.

I will give prompts for reflective writing and how it can positively impact your mindfulness and well-being. However, reflective writing cannot be a one-and-done. Or "I wrote last week, I am good." It should be something that becomes part of your **daily** routine and can be done in less than 5 minutes. And I know we all have 5 minutes. I mean, for real, how long did you spend scrolling social media… decrease that by 5 minutes. And now use that 5-minutes to pull out this book for some personal reflection and well-being.

You can journal in any way that you want. In a notebook, electronically using your phone notes app, using a Google document, or use voice-to-text in an electronic journal. There is no right or wrong way.

The prompts you use to journal should be meaningful to YOU! For example:

- What brings you joy?

- Describe a place you were happiest.

- Write a letter to someone that you always wanted to thank but never did. (Who is the letter for and why are you thanking them?)

____

____

____

- What are you most proud of and why?

____

____

____

If you want to go beyond what is in this book, here is a suggestion for a more in-depth daily journaling experience.

Try it out. This is what it could look like.

- Make a list of 10-15 goals that you have. There is no limit. They can be simple (for me it was drinking more water every day) to big goals (for me, it was writing a book). But I want you to write 15. It is normally really easy to come up with 3-5 goals and we can normally fumble coming up with another 3-5, but our true dreams and aspirations normally come to light when we stretch ourselves past 10. Pick 1 that you will focus on for the next month. The one that you can and will put effort into EVERY DAY.

1. My #1 goal was to put me first- do things that support me and my well being

2. I also made sure that I had a #2 and #3 goal that I would work toward and one of my action items would reflect my commitment to those goals as well.

- Start each day with the affirmation that speaks to you on how you want to show up TODAY. We see so many on social media that we repost, like, and agree with but then we don't do anything about it. Pick one… write it down. And live by it, just for today. (Side note- don't worry… you can have the same affirmation for days, weeks, months… as long as it is inspiring to you, and you are doing something with it.)

   1. Mine: Every choice is a chance for me to make progress!

- Decide the action you are going to take to live by that affirmation TODAY… **just for today**.

   1. Mine:

      - Spend 30 minutes reading
      - Spend 30 minutes writing
      - Meditate and be physically active 30 minutes

   2. Make a note that I did NOT say "every day" this week or for the next month. These are for just one day… the day I am in.

3. I want to also point out that my action steps may be
    the same for multiple days or weeks. I decide each
    day on what I am going to do for me. And even if it
    was the same as the day before, I write it down. The
    action of writing it down is me making the commit-
    ment to doing them.

- Your Moments of gratitude from the last 24 hours. Be
  specific.

  1. Write about something specific for which you are
      grateful. Elaborate in detail about why you are grate-
      ful for this.

  2. Focus on people or circumstances for whom you are
      grateful. This has a greater impact than focusing on
      material things.

  3. If you find yourself struggling to come up with some-
      thing, consider what your life would be like without
      certain people or things, or reflect on how you have
      managed to avoid a negative outcome or been able
      to turn a challenge into something positive.

  4. Be sure to write about unexpected or surprisingly
      positive things that happen in your life.

- What are your top 3 priorities for today? They don't have
  to be monumental. It can be as simple as "take a shower"
  or "eat lunch". Your top 3 that would make today a success for your well-being. By identifying them at the beginning of your day, you will be more likely to achieve them.

1. _______________________________________

2. _______________________________________

3. _______________________________________

- Have an open section where you can write what you want. Your reflective section can be used for working through something, or a place to just write your thoughts, goals, and concerns.

Other suggestions of things to include or track:

- What time I went to bed and what time I got out of bed
- Water intake
- Activity
- Wins and opportunities

YOU HAVE 5 MINUTES… SPEND IT ON YOU!

Now, onto the next part where I am done sharing my journey and you take the reins as you continue your journey.

There are 4 main sections to this book. They are meant to be a 12-week / 3-month journey. I picked 3-months because that is the timeframe that I use to do an overall assessment of where I am at and make adjustments as needed. There is no such thing as work-life balance in the sense that it is or will always be 50-50. One part of your life will always need more attention, effort, comfort, dedication, action, etc. on any given day. However, I assess my "balance" every 3 months. And if I can say that **on average,** I am close to 50-50 effort in my personal-professional life balance, then I am good where I am. If it is not close to 50-50, I make changes. I have made significant career changes in my life because of journaling and self-reflection. And was it ever worth it! I became more financially at peace and more secure than I was earlier in my career but only because of the role journaling played. I have also made changes in my personal life to bring me (and my family) more joy and peace.

I challenge you to use this journal to achieve balance and peace in your life. And to achieve this, it will require change. Change will be difficult. You will be challenged in ways you never imagined. And at some point, you will doubt yourself. Just know that you have been given everything you need to succeed.

Realize change allows us to grow into who we are supposed to be. And that change allows us to accomplish what we never imagined possible or necessary. I seek new opportunities to grow as a pharmacist, a professor, a parent and a spouse. And if I put my mind to it, I can accomplish amazing things I never imagined. I was once asked to give the alumni speech at my high school alma mater, I was asked to provide insight and wisdom. I knew that was going to be difficult to convey in a speech. But I knew this – change occurs constantly. If I can offer anything, it is that we can respond to change by remembering something I attempt to teach every day of my life, "It is easier to embrace change than to resist change". So, embrace the change to come.

Enjoy the roller-coaster!

Week 1 Prompt to Reflect Upon: You were born into this world a clean slate.

Day 1: Write a 6-word story related to "clean".

____

____

____

Day 2: What do you desire to be?

____

____

____

Day 3: What do you desire to change from the world you were born into compared to what you desire to be?

____

____

____

Day 4: Identify one action item that you are willing to incorporate into your daily routine to help move you forward to achieving what you want.

____

____

____

Day 5: What are you grateful for? How do you show you are grateful?

____

____

____

Day 6: Moments of gratitude from the last 24 hours.

____

____

____

Day 7: Top 3 Priorities for this day

____

____

____

Week 1 Recap:

1. What did you learn about yourself this week?

2. What are you most proud of?

3. What will you continue to do?

4. What will you let go of?

Week 2: Doing the same thing expecting different results will not change your life.

Day 1: Write a 6-word story related to "results".

____

____

____

Day 2: Do something that will change your life. (what is that?)

____

____

____

Day 3: What results are you aiming to create?

____

____

____

Day 4: Are your actions aligned with what you aiming to create?

____

____

____

Day 5: Identify one action item that you are willing to incorporate into your daily routine to help move you forward to achieving what you want.

____

____

____

Day 6: What are you grateful for? How do you show you are grateful?

____

____

____

Day 7: Top 3 Priorities for this day

____

____

____

Week 2 Recap:

1. What did you learn about yourself this week?

____

____

____

2. What are you most proud of?

____

____

____

3. What will you continue to do?

____

____

____

4. What will you let go of?

____

____

____

Week 3: What you believe becomes your reality.

Day 1: Write a 6-word story related to "beliefs".

____

____

____

Day 2: What are your beliefs?

____

____

____

Day 3: What do you desire to do more than anything? Do you
believe that?

____

____

____

Day 4: What do you do that indicates you believe that?

____

____

____

Day 5: Identify one action item that you are willing to incorporate into your daily routine to help move you forward to achieving what you want.

____

____

____

Day 6: What are you grateful for? How do you show you are grateful?

____

____

____

Day 7: Top 3 Priorities for this day

____

____

____

Week 3 Recap:

1. What did you learn about yourself this week?

____

____

____

2. What are you most proud of?

____

____

____

3. What will you continue to do?

____

____

____

4. What will you let go of?

____

____

____

Week 4: What are you waiting for?

Day 1: Write a 6-word story related to "waiting".

____

____

____

Day 2: What can you do to move from waiting to doing? (Brain
dump all the options)

____

____

____

Day 3: Pick one option from yesterday that is reasonable to try
today and try it.

____

____

____

Day 4: How did putting your plan into play feel?

____

____

____

Day 5: Identify one action item that you are willing to incorporate into your daily routine to help move you forward to achieving what you want.

____

____

____

Day 6: What are you grateful for? How do you show you are grateful?

____

____

____

Day 7: Top 3 Priorities for this day

____

____

____

Week 4 Recap:

1. What did you learn about yourself this week?

____

____

____

2. What are you most proud of?

____

____

____

3. What will you continue to do?

____

____

____

4. What will you let go of?

____

____

____

Week 5: Seize the Moment

Day 1: Write a 6-word story related to "the moment".

Day 2: What moment/opportunity awaits you?

Day 3: Describe the moment. The sounds, the smells, who are you with, what are you doing.

Day 4: What can you do to create that moment?

Day 5: Identify one action item that you are willing to incorporate into your daily routine to help move you forward to achieving what you want.

____

____

____

Day 6: What are you grateful for? How do you show you are grateful?

____

____

____

Day 7: Top 3 Priorities for this day

____

____

____

Week 5 Recap:

1. What did you learn about yourself this week?

2. What are you most proud of?

3. What will you continue to do?

4. What will you let go of?

Week 6: Who do you inspire to be?

Day 1: Write a 6-word story related to "inspiration".

____

____

____

Day 2: How do you want others to describe you?

____

____

____

Day 3: How do you inspire yourself?

____

____

____

Day 4: What do you need to do or who do you need to connect
with to support you in your journey to becoming YOU?

____

____

____

Day 5: Identify one action item that you are willing to incorporate into your daily routine to help move you forward to achieving what you want.

____

____

____

Day 6: What are you grateful for? How do you show you are grateful?

____

____

____

Day 7: Top 3 Priorities for this day

____

____

____

Week 6 Recap:

1. What did you learn about yourself this week?

2. What are you most proud of?

3. What will you continue to do?

4. What will you let go of?

Week 7: Love

Day 1: Write a 6-word story related to "love".

____

____

____

Day 2: Describe what love is to you.

____

____

____

Day 3: Where does love show up in your life?

____

____

____

Day 4: What can YOU do to show love?

____

____

____

Day 5: Identify one action item that you are willing to incorporate into your daily routine to help move you forward to achieving what you want.

____

____

____

Day 6: What are you grateful for? How do you show you are grateful?

____

____

____

Day 7: Top 3 Priorities for this day

____

____

____

Week 7 Recap:

1. What did you learn about yourself this week?

____

____

____

2. What are you most proud of?

____

____

____

3. What will you continue to do?

____

____

____

4. What will you let go of?

____

____

____

Week 8: Your happy place

Day 1: Write a 6-word story related to "happy".

____

____

____

Day 2: Describe that place. Is it an actual place or a feeling?

____

____

____

Day 3: What can you do to recreate that feeling in other places in your life?

____

____

____

Day 4: Where do you go for happiness, solitude, inspiration, etc.?

____

____

____

Day 5: Identify one action item that you are willing to incorporate into your daily routine to help move you forward to achieving what you want.

____

____

____

Day 6: What are you grateful for? How do you show you are grateful?

____

____

____

Day 7: Top 3 Priorities for this day

____

____

____

Week 8 Recap:

1. What did you learn about yourself this week?

____

____

____

2. What are you most proud of?

____

____

____

3. What will you continue to do?

____

____

____

4. What will you let go of?

____

____

____

Week 9: Be foolish- do what you want to do to improve.

Day 1: Write a 6-word story related to "foolishness".

____

____

____

Day 2: What is that you want so bad but those around you would think you are being a fool?

____

____

____

Day 3: What do you need in order to do that thing?

____

____

____

Day 4: Why is "being a fool" stopping you from following your dream?

____

____

____

Day 5: Identify one action item that you are willing to incorporate into your daily routine to help move you forward to achieving what you want.

____

____

____

Day 6: What are you grateful for? How do you show you are grateful?

____

____

____

Day 7: Top 3 Priorities for this day

____

____

____

Week 9 Recap:

1. What did you learn about yourself this week?

____

____

____

2. What are you most proud of?

____

____

____

3. What will you continue to do?

____

____

____

4. What will you let go of?

____

____

____

Week 10: Light up your life- what lights your fire?

Day 1: Write a 6-word story related to "light".

____

____

____

Day 2: When you light up and can't stop talking about something… what is that you are talking about?

____

____

____

Day 3: What is it about that thing that brings you such joy?

____

____

____

Day 4: What can you do to add that joy to other areas of your
life?

____

____

____

Day 5: Identify one action item that you are willing to incorporate into your daily routine to help move you forward to achieving what you want.

____

____

____

Day 6: What are you grateful for? How do you show you are grateful?

____

____

____

Day 7: Top 3 Priorities for this day

____

____

____

Week 10 Recap:

1. What did you learn about yourself this week?

____

____

____

2. What are you most proud of?

____

____

____

3. What will you continue to do?

____

____

____

4. What will you let go of?

____

____

____

Week 11: Hustle (not just work, but life)

Day 1: Write a 6-word story related to "hustle".

____

____

____

Day 2: What does "hustle" look and feel like?

____

____

____

Day 3: How do you want your family/friends to describe you?

____

____

____

Day 4: Does that description "fill your bucket"?

____

____

____

Day 5: Identify one action item that you are willing to incorporate into your daily routine to help move you forward to achieving what you want.

____

____

____

Day 6: What are you grateful for? How do you show you are grateful?

____

____

____

Day 7: Top 3 Priorities for this day

____

____

____

Week 11 Recap:

1. What did you learn about yourself this week?

____

____

____

2. What are you most proud of?

____

____

____

3. What will you continue to do?

____

____

____

4. What will you let go of?

____

____

____

Week 12: Say you will and then DO IT

Day 1: Write a 6-word story related to "DO IT".

____

____

____

Day 2: What did you say you were going to do week 1? What
steps did you take to do it?

____

____

____

Day 3: What is your next step to make progress?

____

____

____

Day 4: Modify your goal.

____

____

____

Day 5: Identify one action item that you are willing to incorporate into your daily routine to help move you forward to achieving what you want.

____

____

____

Day 6: What are you grateful for? How do you show you are grateful?

____

____

____

Day 7: Top 3 Priorities for this day

____

____

____

Week 12 Recap:

1. What did you learn about yourself this week?

____

____

____

2. What are you most proud of?

____

____

____

3. What will you continue to do?

____

____

____

4. What will you let go of?

____

____

____

12-week Recap

Reflect on your journey.

____

____

____

How did if feel to give yourself 5-minutes every day?

____

____

____

By setting your intentions, did you follow through on your action steps?

____

____

____

What area of your life did you have the most growth?

____

____

____

What area do you want to focus on in the next 3-months?

____

____

____

Week 1: Accomplishment

Day 1: Write a 6-word story related to "accomplishment".

____

____

____

Day 2: What are your current accomplishments?

____

____

____

Day 3: What does accomplishment mean to you?

____

____

____

Day 4: What else do you want to accomplish?

____

____

____

Day 5: Identify one action item that you are willing to incorporate into your daily routine to help move you forward to achieving what you want.

____

____

____

Day 6: What are you grateful for? How do you show you are grateful?

____

____

____

Day 7: Top 3 Priorities for this day

____

____

____

Week 1 Recap:

1. What did you learn about yourself this week?

____

____

____

2. What are you most proud of?

____

____

____

3. What will you continue to do?

____

____

____

4. What will you let go of?

____

____

____

Week 2: Get there

Day 1: Write a 6-word story related to "progress".

____

____

____

Day 2: If you were to tell one person about your goal, what you have been doing and what you plan on doing, what would you say.

____

____

____

Day 3: If you ask someone, "what else can I do?", we often already have an idea in our head of what we want them to say. What would they say on how you can get to your goal?

____

____

____

Day 4: What did your younger self imaging you would be doing at your current age? Compare, contrast. Do you still
want that?

____

____

____

Day 5: Identify one action item that you are willing to incorporate into your daily routine to help move you forward to
achieving what you want.

____

____

____

Day 6: What are you grateful for? How do you show you are
grateful?

____

____

____

Day 7: Top 3 Priorities for this day

____

____

____

Week 2 Recap:

1. What did you learn about yourself this week?

____

____

____

2. What are you most proud of?

____

____

____

3. What will you continue to do?

____

____

____

4. What will you let go of?

____

____

____

Week 3: Who is your support network?

Day 1: Write a 6-word story related to "support".

____

____

____

Day 2: What do you always "thank" others for? And what do others always "thank" you for?

____

____

____

Day 3: Who do you go to now for guidance and support? (can be more than one person… think of it as a "Board of Directors"). How do they support and encourage you? How are you going to maintain connection with those you identified?

____

____

____

Day 4: Who comes to you for guidance and support? What role are you playing?

____

____

____

Day 5: Identify one action item that you are willing to incorporate into your daily routine to help move you forward to achieving what you want.

____

____

____

Day 6: What are you grateful for? How do you show you are grateful?

____

____

____

Day 7: Top 3 Priorities for this day

____

____

____

Week 3 Recap:

1. What did you learn about yourself this week?

____

____

____

2. What are you most proud of?

____

____

____

3. What will you continue to do?

____

____

____

4. What will you let go of?

____

____

____

Week 4: Only you have the answer to your life.

Day 1: Write a 6-word story related to "my life".

____

____

____

Day 2: What makes you smile?

____

____

____

Day 3: What would you regret not having in your life? (person, thing, memory, experience, opportunity, etc..)

____

____

____

Day 4: What is something about you that most people don't know that would surprise them.

____

____

____

Day 5: Identify one action item that you are willing to incorporate into your daily routine to help move you forward to achieving what you want.

____

____

____

Day 6: What are you grateful for? How do you show you are grateful?

____

____

____

Day 7: Top 3 Priorities for this day

____

____

____

Week 4 Recap:

1. What did you learn about yourself this week?

____

____

____

2. What are you most proud of?

____

____

____

3. What will you continue to do?

____

____

____

4. What will you let go of?

____

____

____

Week 5: Take ownership

Day 1: Write a 6-word story related to "ownership".

____

____

____

Day 2: Don't explain what lead you to where you are. Write how you are going to get where you are going.

____

____

____

Day 3: What is your "theme" song?

____

____

____

Day 4: What would you do if you knew you couldn't fail?

____

____

____

Day 5: Identify one action item that you are willing to incorporate into your daily routine to help move you forward to achieving what you want.

____

____

____

Day 6: What are you grateful for? How do you show you are grateful?

____

____

____

Day 7: Top 3 Priorities for this day

____

____

____

Week 5 Recap:

1. What did you learn about yourself this week?

2. What are you most proud of?

3. What will you continue to do?

4. What will you let go of?

Week 6: Change your mindset.

Day 1: Write a 6-word story related to "change".

____

____

____

Day 2: Say "I CAN DO THIS." Write about what "this" is.

____

____

____

Day 3: What do you love to learn about? How did that influence what you do or what you want to do?

____

____

____

Day 4: What could you do all day long that you would not view as a waste of time.

____

____

____

Day 5: Identify one action item that you are willing to incorporate into your daily routine to help move you forward to achieving what you want.

____

____

____

Day 6: What are you grateful for? How do you show you are grateful?

____

____

____

Day 7: Top 3 Priorities for this day

____

____

____

Week 6 Recap:

1. What did you learn about yourself this week?

____

____

____

2. What are you most proud of?

____

____

____

3. What will you continue to do?

____

____

____

4. What will you let go of?

____

____

____

Week 7: Turn off the noise.

Day 1: Write a 6-word story related to "noise".

____

____

____

Day 2: Your action is the only thing that matters. Not your thoughts. What do your actions say about what is important to you?

____

____

____

Day 3: Walk around your home. What would your home say about the things that are important to you?

____

____

____

Day 4: Turn off the noise. What are you going to do by not caring what others think or say about your goals and dreams?

____

____

____

Day 5: Identify one action item that you are willing to incorporate into your daily routine to help move you forward to achieving what you want.

____

____

____

Day 6: What are you grateful for? How do you show you are grateful?

____

____

____

Day 7: Top 3 Priorities for this day

____

____

____

Week 7 Recap:

1. What did you learn about yourself this week?

    ____

    ____

    ____

2. What are you most proud of?

    ____

    ____

    ____

3. What will you continue to do?

    ____

    ____

    ____

4. What will you let go of?

    ____

    ____

    ____

Week 8: Pain and Difficulty… pick different adjectives.

Day 1: Write a 6-word story related to "perseverance".

____

____

____

Day 2: What are your words?

____

____

____

Day 3: What is a job you would do even if you never made any money doing it? How can you do this (even just a little bit) to bring you joy?

____

____

____

Day 4: What are you avoiding doing because it is hard or scary?

____

____

____

Day 5: Identify one action item that you are willing to incorporate into your daily routine to help move you forward to achieving what you want.

____

____

____

Day 6: What are you grateful for? How do you show you are grateful?

____

____

____

Day 7: Top 3 Priorities for this day

____

____

____

Week 8 Recap:

1. What did you learn about yourself this week?

____

____

____

2. What are you most proud of?

____

____

____

3. What will you continue to do?

____

____

____

4. What will you let go of?

____

____

____

Week 9: Home isn't where you are from. It is where you belong.

Day 1: Write a 6-word story related to "home".

____

____

____

Day 2: Where do you belong?

____

____

____

Day 3: What does the road you need to travel look like?

____

____

____

Day 4: Who are you with when you feel most alive?

____

____

____

Day 5: Identify one action item that you are willing to incorporate into your daily routine to help move you forward to achieving what you want.

____

____

____

Day 6: What are you grateful for? How do you show you are grateful?

____

____

____

Day 7: Top 3 Priorities for this day

____

____

____

Week 9 Recap:

1. What did you learn about yourself this week?

____

____

____

2. What are you most proud of?

____

____

____

3. What will you continue to do?

____

____

____

4. What will you let go of?

____

____

____

Week 10: Your expectations derail you. Don't lower your expectations. Have realistic ones.

Day 1: Write a 6-word story related to "expectations".

____

____

____

Day 2: What are your expectations? (pick one area of your life for this initial journaling, you can come back and do it again for other areas)

____

____

____

Day 3: Are your expectations aligned with your actions?

____

____

____

Day 4: How do you hold yourself accountable? How do you know if you are making progress on your expectations/ goals?

____

____

____

Day 5: Identify one action item that you are willing to incorporate into your daily routine to help move you forward to achieving what you want.

____

____

____

Day 6: What are you grateful for? How do you show you are grateful?

____

____

____

Day 7: Top 3 Priorities for this day

____

____

____

Week 10 Recap:

1. What did you learn about yourself this week?

\
\
\

2. What are you most proud of?

\
\
\

3. What will you continue to do?

\
\
\

4. What will you let go of?

\
\
\

Week 11: Being angry only punishes yourself for someone else's mistake. Let it go.

Day 1: Write a 6-word story related to "mistakes".

____

____

____

Day 2: Brain dump on a piece of paper about what you are angry about- feelings/thoughts/actions. How did that feel to let it out?

____

____

____

Day 3: If you could create your own career trajectory, what would it be?

____

____

____

Day 4: Where do you want to be?

____

____

____

Day 5: Identify one action item that you are willing to incorporate into your daily routine to help move you forward to achieving what you want.

____

____

____

Day 6: What are you grateful for? How do you show you are grateful?

____

____

____

Day 7: Top 3 Priorities for this day

____

____

____

Week 11 Recap:

1. What did you learn about yourself this week?

____

____

____

2. What are you most proud of?

____

____

____

3. What will you continue to do?

____

____

____

4. What will you let go of?

____

____

____

Week 12: Your energy creates the reality you desire.

Day 1: Write a 6-word story related to "energy".

____

____

____

Day 2: What is your energy level? What reality do you currently live? Are they reflective of each other?

____

____

____

Day 3: If you could create your own job, what would it be?

____

____

____

Day 4: What is one thing you find time to do *regularly* no matter what?

____

____

____

Day 5: Identify one action item that you are willing to incorporate into your daily routine to help move you forward to achieving what you want.

____

____

____

Day 6: What are you grateful for? How do you show you are grateful?

____

____

____

Day 7: Top 3 Priorities for this day

____

____

____

Week 12 Recap:

1. What did you learn about yourself this week?

____

____

____

2. What are you most proud of?

____

____

____

3. What will you continue to do?

____

____

____

4. What will you let go of?

____

____

____

12-week Recap

Reflect on your journey.

____

____

____

How did if feel to give yourself 5-minutes every day?

____

____

____

By setting your intentions, did you follow through on your action steps?

____

____

____

What area of your life did you have the most growth?

____

____

____

What area do you want to focus on in the next 3-months?

____

____

____

Week 1: As you travel down the river of life, don't use all your strength to hold onto a rock. Life shouldn't be that hard. Continue to travel to the point that requires little energy- that's where you should be.

Day 1: Write a 6-word story related to "flow".

____

____

____

Day 2: Describe how you are flowing down the river. It is easy? Do you need to let go?

____

____

____

Day 3: Would the thing you desire most change how you flow?

____

____

____

Day 4: What is a quote that inspires you? And why?

____

____

____

Day 5: Identify one action item that you are willing to incorporate into your daily routine to help move you forward to
achieving what you want.

____

____

____

Day 6: What are you grateful for? How do you show you are
grateful?

____

____

____

Day 7: Top 3 Priorities for this day

____

____

____

Week 1 Recap:

1. What did you learn about yourself this week?

2. What are you most proud of?

3. What will you continue to do?

4. What will you let go of?

Week 2: Don't apologize for what you want.

Day 1: Write a 6-word story related to "sorry".

____

____

____

Day 2: Write an apology to yourself.

____

____

____

Day 3: When do you apologize? Did you actually do something that warrants an apology?

____

____

____

Day 4: Come up with alternatives of what you will say instead of "I'm sorry" when an apology is not needed.

____

____

____

Day 5: Identify one action item that you are willing to incorporate into your daily routine to help move you forward to achieving what you want.

____

____

____

Day 6: What are you grateful for? How do you show you are grateful?

____

____

____

Day 7: Top 3 Priorities for this day

____

____

____

Week 2 Recap:

1. What did you learn about yourself this week?

____

____

____

2. What are you most proud of?

____

____

____

3. What will you continue to do?

____

____

____

4. What will you let go of?

____

____

____

Week 3: No one is going to promote you like YOU.

Day 1: Write a 6-word story related to "promote".

____

____

____

Day 2: Ask for what you want. Write your ask.

____

____

____

Day 3: You are in the elevator with your idol. Write your 30-90 second elevator speech to promote yourself.

____

____

____

Day 4: Who do you need to share your elevator speech with?

____

____

____

Day 5: Identify one action item that you are willing to incorporate into your daily routine to help move you forward to achieving what you want.

____

____

____

Day 6: What are you grateful for? How do you show you are grateful?

____

____

____

Day 7: Top 3 Priorities for this day

____

____

____

Week 3 Recap:

1. What did you learn about yourself this week?

    ____

    ____

    ____

2. What are you most proud of?

    ____

    ____

    ____

3. What will you continue to do?

    ____

    ____

    ____

4. What will you let go of?

    ____

    ____

    ____

Week 4: Do something fun… regularly.

Day 1: Write a 6-word story related to "play".

____

____

____

Day 2: As kindergarteners, we are given crayons. As we enter our teen years, we are given a pencil (gray-scale). What can you do to bring color back into your days?

____

____

____

Day 3: If you could be any superhero, who would you be and why?

____

____

____

Day 4: You were someone before you are who you are today. What is something you loved doing BEFORE? Did you play a sport, an instrument, sing, draw, play games, volunteer… what did you love doing that you haven't done in a long time. Write it down AND do that!

____

____

____

Day 5: Identify one action item that you are willing to incorporate into your daily routine to help move you forward to achieving what you want.

____

____

____

Day 6: What are you grateful for? How do you show you are grateful?

____

____

____

Day 7: Top 3 Priorities for this day

____

____

____

Week 4 Recap:

1. What did you learn about yourself this week?

____

____

____

2. What are you most proud of?

____

____

____

3. What will you continue to do?

____

____

____

4. What will you let go of?

____

____

____

Week 5: We tell stories to support our actions (how we show up).

Day 1: Write a 6-word story related to "our actions".

____

____

____

Day 2: What story are you telling yourself? What else could be true?

____

____

____

Day 3: What else do you need to know/explore?

____

____

____

Day 4: Do you have FACTS to support your story? What is the real story?

____

____

____

Day 5: Identify one action item that you are willing to incorporate into your daily routine to help move you forward to achieving what you want.

Day 6: What are you grateful for? How do you show you are grateful?

Day 7: Top 3 Priorities for this day

Week 5 Recap:

1. What did you learn about yourself this week?

2. What are you most proud of?

3. What will you continue to do?

4. What will you let go of?

Week 6: Be where your feet are.

Day 1: Write a 6-word story related to "now".

____

____

____

Day 2: Where are your feet now?

____

____

____

Day 3: Where should they be?

____

____

____

Day 4: What story are you telling yourself regarding where your attention is given? How can you realign your attention to where you are now?

____

____

____

Day 5: Identify one action item that you are willing to incorporate into your daily routine to help move you forward to achieving what you want.

____

____

____

Day 6: What are you grateful for? How do you show you are grateful?

____

____

____

Day 7: Top 3 Priorities for this day

____

____

____

Week 6 Recap:

1. What did you learn about yourself this week?

____

____

____

2. What are you most proud of?

____

____

____

3. What will you continue to do?

____

____

____

4. What will you let go of?

____

____

____

Week 7: When someone tells you "You lack confidence" please know that they are threatened by you and trying to knock you down to elevate themselves.

Day 1: Write a 6-word story related to "confidence".

____

____

____

Day 2: When you read that, what is your immediate response?

____

____

____

Day 3: How do you show up (or want to show up) when/if this happens. Do THAT.

____

____

____

Day 4: How do you support others?

____

____

____

Day 5: Identify one action item that you are willing to incorporate into your daily routine to help move you forward to
achieving what you want.

____

____

____

Day 6: What are you grateful for? How do you show you are
grateful?

____

____

____

Day 7: Top 3 Priorities for this day

____

____

____

Week 7 Recap:

1. What did you learn about yourself this week?

____

____

____

2. What are you most proud of?

____

____

____

3. What will you continue to do?

____

____

____

4. What will you let go of?

____

____

____

Week 8: You have strengths/skills you don't know you have (or that you haven't used in a while).

Day 1: Write a 6-word story related to "skills".

____

____

____

Day 2: What are your strengths and how do you know those are your strengths?

____

____

____

Day 3: What is something you are good at (and it helps if you like doing it too) that you don't get to do often in your personal or professional life?

____

____

____

Day 4: What can you do so you do more of it?

____

____

____

Day 5: Identify one action item that you are willing to incorporate into your daily routine to help move you forward to achieving what you want.

____

____

____

Day 6: What are you grateful for? How do you show you are grateful?

____

____

____

Day 7: Top 3 Priorities for this day

____

____

____

Week 8 Recap:

1. What did you learn about yourself this week?

____

____

____

2. What are you most proud of?

____

____

____

3. What will you continue to do?

____

____

____

4. What will you let go of?

____

____

____

Week 9: Remove one thing from the world

Day 1: Write a 6-word story related to "simplicity".

____

____

____

Day 2: What would you remove and why?

____

____

____

Day 3: If said thing no longer existed, how would that improve
your life?

____

____

____

Day 4: What are you going to do to lead the way in removing
that one thing?

____

____

____

Day 5: Identify one action item that you are willing to incorporate into your daily routine to help move you forward to achieving what you want.

____

____

____

Day 6: What are you grateful for? How do you show you are grateful?

____

____

____

Day 7: Top 3 Priorities for this day

____

____

____

Week 9 Recap:

1. What did you learn about yourself this week?

____

____

____

2. What are you most proud of?

____

____

____

3. What will you continue to do?

____

____

____

4. What will you let go of?

____

____

____

Week 10: Good relationships keep us happier and healthier.

Day 1: Write a 6-word story related to "relationships".

____

____

____

Day 2: What relationship is good/solid and makes you the happiest?

____

____

____

Day 3: What relationship(s) do you want to keep that need(s) to be repaired… how are you going to pave the way to repair it? Reminder- it is a 2-way street. The burden of a solid relationship does not fall on one person's shoulder, BUT we need to our part.

____

____

____

Day 4: How are you going to keep your strong relationships strong?

____

____

____

Day 5: Identify one action item that you are willing to incorporate into your daily routine to help move you forward to achieving what you want.

____

____

____

Day 6: What are you grateful for? How do you show you are grateful?

____

____

____

Day 7: Top 3 Priorities for this day

____

____

____

Week 10 Recap:

1. What did you learn about yourself this week?

____

____

____

2. What are you most proud of?

____

____

____

3. What will you continue to do?

____

____

____

4. What will you let go of?

____

____

____

Week 11: Maintain/Improve the quality of the relationships that are most important to you.

Day 1: Write a 6-word story related to "quality".

Day 2: List 3 relationships (personal, friend, and colleague)

Day 3: How do you need them to show-up for you? Do they? What can you do to let them know what you need?

Day 4: How do you show-up for them?

Day 5: Identify one action item that you are willing to incorporate into your daily routine to help move you forward to achieving what you want.

____

____

____

Day 6: What are you grateful for? How do you show you are grateful?

____

____

____

Day 7: Top 3 Priorities for this day

____

____

____

Week 11 Recap:

1. What did you learn about yourself this week?

____

____

____

2. What are you most proud of?

____

____

____

3. What will you continue to do?

____

____

____

4. What will you let go of?

____

____

____

Week 12: Be a teacher to others.

Day 1: Write a 6-word story related to "teacher".

____

____

____

Day 2: What are 5 characteristics of the best "teacher" you ever
had?

____

____

____

Day 3: How do you want other to describe you as a "teacher"?

____

____

____

Day 4: What do you want to teach?

____

____

____

Day 5: Identify one action item that you are willing to incorporate into your daily routine to help move you forward to achieving what you want.

____

____

____

Day 6: What are you grateful for? How do you show you are grateful?

____

____

____

Day 7: Top 3 Priorities for this day

____

____

____

Week 12 Recap:

1. What did you learn about yourself this week?

____

____

____

2. What are you most proud of?

____

____

____

3. What will you continue to do?

____

____

____

4. What will you let go of?

____

____

____

12-week Recap

Reflect on your journey.

____

____

____

How did if feel to give yourself 5-minutes every day?

____

____

____

By setting your intentions, did you follow through on your action steps?

____

____

____

What area of your life did you have the most growth?

____

____

____

What area do you want to focus on in the next 3-months?

____

____

____

You are 9 months into journaling. The last 3 months I am just providing the weekly prompt. You decide what to write based on the prompt. No direct questions to answer. How does it make you feel? What speaks to you the most about the prompt? Write your 6-word story related to the prompt. Day 2-4 are up to you on how you approach the prompt. Day 5 is your action item, Day 6 is what you are grateful for, and day 7 is your top 3 priorities related to the prompt.

Week 1: Make your voice be heard.

Day 1: Write your 6-word story.

____

____

____

Day 2-4: Write on what you want as long as it relates to the prompt.

Day 2:

____

____

____

Day 3:

____

____

____

Day 4:

____

____

____

Day 5: Identify one action item that you are willing to incorporate into your daily routine to help move you forward to achieving what you want.

____

____

____

Day 6: What are you grateful for? How do you show you are grateful?

____

____

____

Day 7: Top 3 Priorities for this day

____

____

____

Week 1 Recap:

1. What did you learn about yourself this week?

____

____

____

2. What are you most proud of?

____

____

____

3. What will you continue to do?

____

____

____

4. What will you let go of?

____

____

____

Week 2: Back to basics- what are your pillars of health and how do you support them.

Day 1: Write your 6-word story.

____

____

____

Day 2-4: Write on what you want as long as it relates to the prompt.

Day 2:

____

____

____

Day 3:

____

____

____

Day 4:

____

____

____

Day 5: Identify one action item that you are willing to incorporate into your daily routine to help move you forward to achieving what you want.

____

____

____

Day 6: What are you grateful for? How do you show you are grateful?

____

____

____

Day 7: Top 3 Priorities for this day

____

____

____

Week 2 Recap:

1. What did you learn about yourself this week?

2. What are you most proud of?

3. What will you continue to do?

4. What will you let go of?

Week 3: Identify your personal board of directors that can support you in your journey

Day 1: Write your 6-word story.

____

____

____

Day 2-4: Write on what you want as long as it relates to the prompt.

Day 2:

____

____

____

Day 3:

____

____

____

Day 4:

____

____

____

Day 5: Identify one action item that you are willing to incorporate into your daily routine to help move you forward to achieving what you want.

____

____

____

Day 6: What are you grateful for? How do you show you are grateful?

____

____

____

Day 7: Top 3 Priorities for this day

____

____

____

Week 3 Recap:

1. What did you learn about yourself this week?

____

____

____

2. What are you most proud of?

____

____

____

3. What will you continue to do?

____

____

____

4. What will you let go of?

____

____

____

Week 4: Set boundaries to advocate for yourself regardless of how others respond

Day 1: Write your 6-word story.

____

____

____

Day 2-4: Write on what you want as long as it relates to the prompt.

Day 2:

____

____

____

Day 3:

____

____

____

Day 4:

____

____

____

Day 5: Identify one action item that you are willing to incorporate into your daily routine to help move you forward to achieving what you want.

____

____

____

Day 6: What are you grateful for? How do you show you are grateful?

____

____

____

Day 7: Top 3 Priorities for this day

____

____

____

Week 4 Recap:

1. What did you learn about yourself this week?

____

____

____

2. What are you most proud of?

____

____

____

3. What will you continue to do?

____

____

____

4. What will you let go of?

____

____

____

Week 5: Think more than you say

Day 1: Write your 6-word story.

____

____

____

Day 2-4: Write on what you want as long as it relates to the
        prompt.

Day 2:

____

____

____

Day 3:

____

____

____

Day 4:

____

____

____

Day 5: Identify one action item that you are willing to incorporate into your daily routine to help move you forward to achieving what you want.

____

____

____

Day 6: What are you grateful for? How do you show you are grateful?

____

____

____

Day 7: Top 3 Priorities for this day

____

____

____

Week 5 Recap:

1. What did you learn about yourself this week?

____

____

____

2. What are you most proud of?

____

____

____

3. What will you continue to do?

____

____

____

4. What will you let go of?

____

____

____

Week 6: Listen more than you talk.

Day 1: Write your 6-word story.

____

____

____

Day 2-4: Write on what you want as long as it relates to the
prompt.

Day 2:

____

____

____

Day 3:

____

____

____

Day 4:

____

____

____

Day 5: Identify one action item that you are willing to incorporate into your daily routine to help move you forward to achieving what you want.

____

____

____

Day 6: What are you grateful for? How do you show you are grateful?

____

____

____

Day 7: Top 3 Priorities for this day

____

____

____

Week 6 Recap:

1. What did you learn about yourself this week?

____

____

____

2. What are you most proud of?

____

____

____

3. What will you continue to do?

____

____

____

4. What will you let go of?

____

____

____

Week 7: If you don't ask, the answer is always no.

Day 1: Write your 6-word story.

____

____

____

Day 2-4: Write on what you want as long as it relates to the
        prompt.

Day 2:

____

____

____

Day 3:

____

____

____

Day 4:

____

____

____

Day 5: Identify one action item that you are willing to incorporate into your daily routine to help move you forward to achieving what you want.

____

____

____

Day 6: What are you grateful for? How do you show you are grateful?

____

____

____

Day 7: Top 3 Priorities for this day

____

____

____

Week 7 Recap:

1. What did you learn about yourself this week?

    \
    \
    \

2. What are you most proud of?

    \
    \
    \

3. What will you continue to do?

    \
    \
    \

4. What will you let go of?

    \
    \
    \

Week 8: If you don't step forward, you are always in the same place.

Day 1: Write your 6-word story.

____

____

____

Day 2-4: Write on what you want as long as it relates to the prompt.

Day 2:

____

____

____

Day 3:

____

____

____

Day 4:

____

____

____

Day 5: Identify one action item that you are willing to incorporate into your daily routine to help move you forward to achieving what you want.

____

____

____

Day 6: What are you grateful for? How do you show you are grateful?

____

____

____

Day 7: Top 3 Priorities for this day

____

____

____

Week 8 Recap:

1. What did you learn about yourself this week?

____

____

____

2. What are you most proud of?

____

____

____

3. What will you continue to do?

____

____

____

4. What will you let go of?

____

____

____

Week 9: When things feel overwhelming- remember, one day at a atime, one task at a time, one thought at a time.

Day 1: Write your 6-word story.

____

____

____

Day 2-4: Write on what you want as long as it relates to the prompt.

Day 2:

____

____

____

Day 3:

____

____

____

Day 4:

____

____

____

Day 5: Identify one action item that you are willing to incorporate into your daily routine to help move you forward to achieving what you want.

____

____

____

Day 6: What are you grateful for? How do you show you are grateful?

____

____

____

Day 7: Top 3 Priorities for this day

____

____

____

Week 9 Recap:

1. What did you learn about yourself this week?

____

____

____

2. What are you most proud of?

____

____

____

3. What will you continue to do?

____

____

____

4. What will you let go of?

____

____

____

Week 10: Stress doesn't come from what is going on around you. It comes from your thoughts about what is going on around you. (slightly modifed from an Andrew Berstein quote)

Day 1: Write your 6-word story.

____

____

____

Day 2-4: Write on what you want as long as it relates to the prompt.

Day 2:

____

____

____

Day 3:

____

____

____

Day 4:

____

____

____

Day 5: Identify one action item that you are willing to incorporate into your daily routine to help move you forward to achieving what you want.

____

____

____

Day 6: What are you grateful for? How do you show you are grateful?

____

____

____

Day 7: Top 3 Priorities for this day

____

____

____

Week 10 Recap:

1. What did you learn about yourself this week?

____

____

____

2. What are you most proud of?

____

____

____

3. What will you continue to do?

____

____

____

4. What will you let go of?

____

____

____

Week 11: No amount of guilt can change the past and no amount of anxiety can change the future. (slightly modified from an Umar Ibn Al-Khattab quote)

Day 1: Write your 6-word story.

____

____

____

Day 2-4: Write on what you want as long as it relates to the prompt.

Day 2:

____

____

____

Day 3:

____

____

____

Day 4:

____

____

____

Day 5: Identify one action item that you are willing to incorporate into your daily routine to help move you forward to achieving what you want.

____

____

____

Day 6: What are you grateful for? How do you show you are grateful?

____

____

____

Day 7: Top 3 Priorities for this day

____

____

____

1. What did you learn about yourself this week?

    ____

    ____

    ____

2. What are you most proud of?

    ____

    ____

    ____

3. What will you continue to do?

    ____

    ____

    ____

4. What will you let go of?

    ____

    ____

    ____

Week 12: It is better to walk alone than with a crowd going in the wrong direction. (Herman Su)

Day 1: Write your 6-word story.

____

____

____

Day 2-4: Write on what you want as long as it relates to the prompt.

Day 2:

____

____

____

Day 3:

____

____

____

Day 4:

____

____

____

Day 5: Identify one action item that you are willing to incorporate into your daily routine to help move you forward to achieving what you want.

____

____

____

Day 6: What are you grateful for? How do you show you are grateful?

____

____

____

Day 7: Top 3 Priorities for this day

____

____

____

Week 12 Recap:

1. What did you learn about yourself this week?

____

____

____

2. What are you most proud of?

____

____

____

3. What will you continue to do?

____

____

____

4. What will you let go of?

____

____

____

12-week Recap

Reflect on your journey.

____

____

____

How did if feel to give yourself 5-minutes every day?

____

____

____

By setting your intentions, did you follow through on your action steps?

____

____

____

What area of your life did you have the most growth?

____

____

____

What area do you want to focus on in the next 3-months?

____

____

____

Daily Words for Reflection-

Going forward, you can use these for inspiration in reflective writing as you continue your journey.

Accept	Act	Allow	Appreciate	Balance	Be	Begin
Belong	Boundaries	Break	Breathe	Build	Calm	Care
Challenge	Change	Choice	Close	Commit	Connect	Create
Do	Dream	Embrace	Emerge	Engage	Enjoy	Experience
Feel	Find	Finish	Flow	Focus	Forgive	Give
Heal	Help	Hold	Honor	Hope	Ignore	Imagine
Include	Innovate	Inspire	Invite	Journey	Keep	Laugh
Lead	Learn	Leave	Listen	Live	Make	Meet
Mentor	Move	Need	Nourish	Own	Pause	Play
Practice	Protect	Question	Quit	Reach	Read	Release
Remember	Renew	Respect	Rest	Reward	Say	Separate
Share	Simplify	Share	Sleep	Smile	Stretch	Take
Talk	Teach	Thank	Think	Try	Understand	Unite
Wait	Walk	Whisper	Wonder	Work	Write	Yes
No	Progress	Purpose	Family	Joy	Travel	Wellness

Another writing exercise to work through is exploring your life by answering some very pointed questions. I did this in 2021 and have shared this with my coach, who challenged me further for my personal and professional growth. I have also made this a living (virtual) document, that is reviewed and modified (if needed) every 3 months. If you are up to it, answer these questions for yourself as you continue your journey.

This will be a living document that you can revisit on a regular basis for reflection and fine-tuning.

Create your personal development plan using these questions. Remember, it is a living document and you will probably not answer all of these questions in one setting.

- Who am I?
- Where am I?
- Where do i want to go?
- What is my plan to get there?
- How can I be kept accountable?
- What resources do I require?
- With whom do I need to meet?

**Don't just be good to others.
Be good to yourself, first.**

Contact the Author: DVYOUNGAdvantage@outlook.com

Website: https://dvyoungadvantage.org

www.ingramcontent.com/pod-product-compliance
Lightning Source LLC
Chambersburg PA
CBHW070355301025
34737CB00047B/844